I0814543

THE POCKET

Lana Del Rey

Published in 2025
by Gemini Books
Part of Gemini Books Group

Based in Woodbridge and London

Marine House, Tide Mill Way,
Woodbridge, Suffolk IP12 1AP
United Kingdom
www.geminibooks.com

Part of the Gemini Pockets series

Cover illustration by Natalie Floss

ISBN 978-1-80247-295-0

A CIP catalogue record for this book is available from the British Library.

Manufacturer's EU Representative: Eurolink Compliance Limited, 25 Herbert Place, Dublin, D02 AY86, Republic of Ireland. admin@eurolink-europe.ie.

Printed in China

10 9 8 7 6 5 4 3 2 1

Images: Alamy: 4 / UPI; 7 / Matt Crossick; 46 / Associated Press.
Getty Images: 8 / Joseph Okpako; 74 / Rabbani and Solimene Photography; 100 / Steve Jennings.

THE POCKET

Lana Del Rey

G:

PEACE

CONTENTS

Introduction

A poet disguised as a pop star, Lana Del Rey is as misunderstood as she is mysterious. Since her arrival in the mainstream in 2011, Lana has consistently confounded her fans' expectations and confused her critics, by releasing a relentless string of genre-bending, melodically mesmerizing songs that both defy, and define, modern pop music.

In her decade at the forefront of popular culture, Lana has become an influential muse to many of the world's musical icons, from Taylor Swift to Stevie Nicks, Billie Eilish to Bruce Springsteen.

At the core of our love Lana is her gift for metaphor, melodrama, melody and lyrics; her romantic verse best reveals the real America, with its glamorous but fading façade, both wild and wholesome all in one. A bit like Lana, then.

Chapter One
La Na Land

"If I had to peer right inside my heart, it's really big. And it's really hot and warm. But it can be icy though."

Lana Del Rey, *Harper's Bazaar*, November 2023

Kurt Cobain: King of Sadcore

Growing up in America in the 1980s and '90s meant one thing: you couldn't escape MTV or its 24-hour rotation of music videos.

It was in 1994, when Lana was nine, that she first fell in love with Kurt Cobain, the lead singer of rock band Nirvana. "When I saw Kurt Cobain on *MTV Unplugged* I thought 'Fuck my life! That is so sexy!' He was so much more epic than anyone else I had ever encountered on television, or in real life," Lana told *i-D* in June 2014.

Cobain would remain Lana's biggest influence on her "Sadcore" music, telling SiriusXM in 2011: "When I was 11, I saw Kurt Cobain singing 'Heart-Shaped Box' on MTV and it really stopped me dead in my tracks. I thought he was the most beautiful person I had ever seen. Even at a young age, I really related to his sadness."

Sketchy Schooling

At age 14, in 1999, Lana was sent to Kent School, an all-girl boarding school in Connecticut, USA. Her parents, Richard and Patricia, hoped the move would limit Lana's growing dependence on drugs and alcohol. "I was a big drinker at the time. I would drink alone. I thought the whole concept was so fucking cool. A great deal of what I wrote on *Born to Die* is about these wilderness years," Lana told *GQ* in October 2012.

Unfortunately, while Lana was at Kent School – until aged 18 – it took a while for her to become a "good girl". She frequently skipped classes, got drunk at local dive bars with her gang of schoolgirls and was bullied mercilessly the entire time for being "white trash", events that inspired Lana to write the killer track, 'This Is What Makes Us Girls' from *Born to Die*.

"Freud and Jung say that 30 per cent of what you end up thinking about your own self is based on what other people think of you. I believe that. I make sure I know what my story is. That's why I get mad if I read something that seems off. Because I'm so sure of my story."

Lana Del Rey, *Los Angeles Times*, October 2019

21 June 1985

The summer solstice marks the longest day of the year and Lana Del Rey's birthday.

Somewhat spookily, when Lana was born in 1985, the No. 1 song in the UK was 'You'll Never Walk Alone'. (See the significance on page 93.)

"I was born on the day of the worldly rapture, according to the most famous biblical birthdays, June 21."

Lana Del Rey, *NME*, January 2012

Lake Placid

Lana may be the epitome of Californian cool, but she was actually born and raised in a tiny upstate New York town – Lake Placid.

1. The American word holiday – "vacation" – was invented to describe Lake Placid by wealthy New York families who would "vacate" the dirty big city to the town's fresh mountain air.

2. Lake Placid is consistently voted the No. 1 town in America to celebrate Halloween.

3. The Adirondacks is one of the largest protected natural areas in America. It's an area so big that it could fit the natural parks of Yosemite, Great Smoky Mountains, Yellowstone and the Grand Canyon inside it.

4. Lake Placid "America's first winter resort", is the first and only US host of the Winter Olympics.

5. The 1999 movie *Lake Placid*, about a giant crocodile that terrorizes the small town community, remains a cult classic.

"When I was very young I was floored by the fact that my mother and my father and everyone I knew was going to die one day – and myself too. I couldn't believe that we were mortal. For some reason that knowledge sort of overshadowed my experience. I was unhappy for some time. I got into a lot of trouble. I used to drink a lot. That was a hard time in my life. I had a philosophical crisis."

Lana Del Rey, *The Daily Telegraph*, January 2012

In January 2012, after two years of writing and recording with producer Emile Haynie and co-writer Justin Parker, Lana finally released her first major label debut album after two false start records.

Born to Die was heaped with commercial and critical acclaim, selling more than 7 million copies.

Most importantly, it changed the musical landscape for emerging female artists, opening the door for artists such as Taylor Swift, Billie Eilish and Miley Cyrus to be true to themselves.

Essential Album #1:

Born to Die

1. 'Born to Die'
2. 'Off to the Races'
3. 'Blue Jeans'
4. 'Video Games'
5. 'Diet Mountain Dew'
6 'National Anthem'
7. 'Dark Paradise'
8. 'Radio'
9. 'Carmen'
10. 'Million Dollar Man'
11. 'Summertime Sadness'
12. 'This Is What Makes Us Girls'

"I wanted a name as beautiful as the music. I was going to Miami quite a lot at the time, speaking a lot of Spanish with my friends from Cuba. 'Lana Del Rey' reminded us of the glamour of the seaside. It sounded gorgeous coming off the tip of the tongue."

Lana Del Rey, *Vogue*, October 2011

Lana Turner

During the recording of her debut album *Lana Del Ray AKA Lizzie Grant*, in 2010 (with super-producer David Kahne), Elizabeth Woolridge Grant changed her name to the stage name, Lana Del Ray, inspired by Old Hollywood icon Lana Turner and the Del Rey, a popular model of car made by the Ford Motor Company.

An icon of the Golden Age of Cinema in the 1940s and '50s, the original femme fatale Lana Turner was famed for her dramatic roles – and even more dramatic personal life. (She married eight times, and her daughter, Cheryl, fatally stabbed one of Turner's abusive boyfriends.) Our Lana's looks are heavily influenced by this stunning star of the silver screen, as well the origin of her name.

"Never had a persona. Never needed one. Never will."

Lana Del Rey, *The Atlantic*, September 2019

Always Authentic

Since her very first major-league interview in 2011, Lana has been accused of being a prop, a fake and not a genuine artist, something that angers Lana greatly.

"After the first person wrote about me, the articles became just blatant, all-out lies. I consider it slander. If I cared more, I'd kill them," she told *Electronic Beats* in June 2013.

"I'll never forget my first four years of interviews. They just fucking burned me."

Lana Del Rey, *Mojo*, June 2023

Metaphysics

After a spell at an all-girl's school in Connecticut where her uncle was a teacher, 18-year-old Lana moved to New York to continue her education. Lana chose to study Metaphysics at Fordham University, located in the Bronx. Lana told *Vogue* in October 2012 that she selected the subject because it "bridged the gap between God and science".

Like Lana's lyrics, metaphysics, a branch of philosophy, tries to understand reality, existence, identity, time and space. "There are different branches of metaphysics," Lana told *i-D* in June 2014, "but my branch studied the origins of the universe and how reality came to be real."

Who's Lizzy?

Before Elizabeth Woolridge Grant AKA Lizzy Grant chose Lana Del Rey (or Ray!) as her final stage name, she also released music online under a few other pseudonyms, including:

Sparkle Jump Rope Queen – check out the 2008 song 'Elvis' still up on MySpace.

May Jailer – the stage name under which she released an album and two EPs.

Lana's parents, brother Charlie and sister Chuck are reportedly the only people who call the singer by her birth name, Lizzy. In an interview with *Pitchfork* in 2017, Lana revealed that even her closest and oldest friends now call her Lana.

18 October 2011

The day Lana's life changed forever. It was the day she posted to Vevo her first self-directed video for 'Video Games'.

After Lana and co-writer Justin Parker penned 'Video Games' in 2010, while she was living in London. Frustrated by her record label's disinterest in the song, Lana chose to upload her own video to see what would happen. "We thought it was really special but the record label didn't. Lana's video just took off. They had to release it then, they had no choice," Parker told the *Independent* in 2012.

The video was a montage of old Hollywood clips spliced with home-made video of Lana. Within 24 hours it had gone viral, receiving more than a million views. On the 25th hour, it was promptly taken down for copyright issues. It's back up now.

Whole Lotta Lana

Unlike many of her solo female contemporaries, Lana is prolific. Incredibly, she has released an album every 18 months, on average, since 2008! With 2021's *Blue Banisters*, there was only a seven-month gap from the preceding album.

1. ***Lana Del Ray AKA Lizzy Grant* (2010)**
2. ***Born to Die* (2012) – 7 million copies!**
3. ***Ultraviolence* (2014)**
4. ***Honeymoon* (2015)**
5. ***Lust for Life* (2017)**
6. ***Norman Fucking Rockwell!* (2019)**
7. ***Chemtrails over the Country Club* (2021)**
8. ***Blue Banisters* (2021)**
9. ***Did You Know That There's a Tunnel Under Ocean Blvd* (2023)**
10. ***The Right Person Will Stay* (2025)**

"I've got an eccentric side when it comes to the muse of writing. I feel very much that writing is not my thing: I'm writing's thing. When the writing has got me, I'm on its schedule. But when it leaves me alone, I'm just at Starbucks, talking shit all day."

Lana Del Rey, *Billboard*, August 2019

41 million

According to Lana's parent record label, Universal Music Group, she has sold more than 41 million albums and has amassed more than 58 billion streams worldwide.

In addition to this, Lana has sold more than 48 million certified singles. This makes Lana the 37th best-selling female solo artist of all time.

Ford Del Rey

The car from which Lana took inspiration for her stage surname was the Ford Del Rey, a model that was manufactured from 1981 to 1991, when Lana was in middle school.

The Del Rey mainly catered to the Brazilian market where it became popular for its comfort and fuel efficiency. In Spanish, "Del Rey" is a phrase that translates to "of the King" in English.

So, arise, Lana… the King!

"When I was aged 18, my uncle taught me six basic chords on the guitar – G, C, A. It was D minor, A minor and some diminished chord as well. I realized I could probably write a million songs with those six chords – so I moved to New York and I took a couple of years to just write whatever I wanted."

Lana Del Rey, BBC News, January 2012

Fordham University

When Lana was 18, she began her first "musical experience" performing at underground folk clubs and venues in New York.

At the same time, she was also studying metaphysics at Fordham University. The university has had many famous alumni from the Arts field, including two-time Oscar winner Denzel Washington, Alan Alda, Patricia Clarkson, Taylor Schilling, Amanda Seyfried, Robert Sean Leonard, Regina Hall, David Copperfield and Faith Evans.

London Lady

In February 2013, Lana walked away with the golden statue for International Female Solo Artist at the Brit Awards, the second Brit Award in a row after her win in 2012 for International Breakthrough Act – the first consecutive win of the International Award. She beat Taylor Swift, Cat Power, Rihanna and Alicia Keys to the prize.

"I was a bad girl, but I'm good now. I guess I have some bad tendencies. I am drawn to the wild side."

Lana Del Rey, *Electronic Beats*, June 2013

Lana's awesome second album, *Ultraviolence*, was the first Lana Del Rey album to debut at the No. 1 spot on the US Billboard charts and the first to incorporate more classic rock influences.

Released on 13 June 2014, the album remains one of Lana's, and her fans', personal favourites.

Essential Album #2:

Ultraviolence

1. 'Cruel World'
2. 'Ultraviolence'
3. 'Shades of Cool'
4. 'Brooklyn Baby'
5. 'West Coast'
6. 'Sad Girl'
7. 'Pretty When You Cry'
8. 'Money Power Glory'
9. 'Fucked My Way Up to the Top'
10. 'Old Money'
11. 'The Other Woman'

Manchester Debut

The short but sweet setlist of Lana's first official concert as Lana Del Rey at The Ruby Lounge, Manchester, UK, on 4 November 2011 included:

1. 'Without You'
2. 'Blue Jeans'
3. 'Video Games'
4. 'Off to the Races'

"My sweet, sweet crowd," she said to the 600-strong audience after 'Blue Jeans'. "I can't take it, it's so nice!"

This performance was the first of her 39-show debut Born to Die Tour, her only club tour. This show sold out in 13 minutes.

Born to Die

The origin of Lana's fascination with the phrase "Born to Die", came from a 2,500-year-old play by the famed Greek tragedy playwright Sophocles. As a child, Lana developed a "death anxiety", or thanatophobia, which led to severe bouts of depression.

"She was a god, born of gods, and we are only mortals born to die. And yet, of course, it's a great thing for a dying girl to hear, just hear she shares a destiny equal to the gods, during life and late, once she's dead."

Sophocles, Chorus, *Antigone*,
Lines 925–930, 441 BCE

Sirens

Lana's debut album *Sirens* was recorded in 2006 when the singer was 21 years old. The album was never officially released but it was mysteriously leaked on YouTube the same month *Born to Die* was released in 2012.

If you've never heard of the album, it's a jamboree of 15 alt-folk tracks, and recorded under a pseudonym – May Jailer. Check out 'How Do You Know Me So Well' – Lana is there underneath. It's beautiful.

"Onstage, I wear the same shoes and dress that I go to lunch in. It's always just a dress off the rack. I do my own makeup. But everyone says I have a 'persona'. Just because I wear short dresses doesn't mean I can't write my own narrative."

Lana Del Rey, *Los Angeles Times*, October 2019

Living a Dream

Following the global success of *Born to Die* and *Ultraviolence*, Lana was arguably the most important female artist on the planet.

With her star at its zenith, the world's biggest movie star, Angelina Jolie, cherry-picked Lana to perform the classic fairytale song 'Once Upon a Dream', as the main theme for Jolie's *Maleficent* (2014). The melody was composed by Tchaikovsky for his 1890 ballet, *The Sleeping Beauty*.

"I make everything for me. Every little thing, right down to the guitar and the drums. It's just for me. I want to hear it, I want to drive to it, I want to swim in the ocean to it. I want to think about it, and then I want to write something new after it."

Lana Del Rey, *Rolling Stone*, July 2014

Under the Influence

Lana wears her influences on the sleeves of her beautiful sundresses. If you really want to get inside Lana's head, check out her favourite songs:

1. 'Falling' – Julee Cruise

2. 'Some Velvet Morning' – Nancy Sinatra

3. 'When I'm Gone' – Eminem

4. 'Love Me Tender' – Elvis Presley

5. 'And I Love Her' – the Beatles

6. 'Hotel California' – the Eagles

7. 'American Beauty' – Thomas Newman

8. 'Love is a Losing Game' – Amy Winehouse

9. 'Walk on the Wild Side' – Lou Reed

10. 'Famous Blue Raincoat' – Leonard Cohen

Like Clockwork

Violence hung heavily in Lana's mind in 2014 when she completed the songwriting on her second record, *Ultraviolence*.

The word "ultraviolence" was first used in Anthony Burgess's iconic 1962 novel *A Clockwork Orange* and Stanley Kubrick's 1971 feature film.

Lana picked the word for the album's title because she liked the "luxe sound of the word 'ultra' and the mean sound of the word 'violence' together," she told the BBC in 2014.

On the album's title track, Lana describes the violence of domestic abuse that so many American women face in relationships today, with Lana pointedly deploying a lyric from the Crystals' 1962 hit, 'He Hit Me (And It Felt Like a Kiss)' to devastating effect. She now refuses to sing that line live.

Chapter Two

Bittersweet Heart

AKA Lizzy Grant

In 2007, while studying at university in New York, Lizzy Grant (AKA Lana Del Ray – note the different spelling of Rey) signed her first record deal for $10,000 with independent New York-based label 5 Points after she submitted a demo tape of acoustic tracks called *No Kung Fu*.

Over the next two years, Lana recorded her first album entitled *Lana Del Ray AKA Lizzy Grant* with producer David Kahne, who'd previously worked with Paul McCartney and Regina Spektor.

The album was never formally released and was removed online by Lana's new managers after she signed a major label record deal with Interscope in 2010. It's now available on YouTube. Definitely check out the first track, 'Kill Kill'.

" I had signed to an independent label but they couldn't fund the release of it. People act like it's so shrouded in mystery, the 'forgotten terrible album'. But if you look on YouTube, all 13 tracks are available with millions of views, so it's not like no one's heard them. It's pretty good. "

Lana Del Rey, BBC News, January 2012

“I found one of my musical soulmates, Justin Parker. He played out some sustained piano chords, and I leaned back and started thinking about one of my favourite times. And that was how, really, the second evolution of my style began.”

Lana Del Rey, *Discopop*, January 2012

Justin Parker

Lana has worked with many co-writers and producers who have helped steer her music toward stardom. The first of these was British songwriter Justin Parker who was paired up with Lana by his publishers, Sony/ATV Music, to work on a few songs in a London studio in 2010.

"I wrote the chord sequence for the verse to 'Video Games' at home and thought 'that sounds like a Lana song to me'," Parker told the *Independent* in 2012. "She wrote the lyrics and the song was all written in three hours."

The duo went on to write another seven songs for the album ***Born to Die***. Parker has since written for other pop elites, including Sia, Linkin Park, Rihanna and Ellie Goulding.

400 Weeks

In addition to being the fifth highest-selling album in the world in 2012, *Born to Die* is also one of just three albums by a female artist – *in the history of pop music* – to spend more than 400 weeks on the US Billboard 200. Can you guess the other two?

Adele (*21*) and Carole King (*Tapestry*).

Trailer Trash

Between 2007 and 2010, as Lana was recording her debut album *Lana Del Ray AKA Lizzie Grant*, the singer moved to a trailer park called Manhattan Mobile Home Park, North Bergen, New Jersey, with her then-boyfriend, Josh Kemp.

It was there, while living as "trailer trash" that Lana felt inspired to write lyrics. "I wrote 'Video Games' after I let go of my ambitions of becoming a noteworthy artist, and was just enjoying being with my boyfriend living in a trailer park, watching him play video games. That was all my life consisted of and I was at peace with that, so to me it's a happy song." Lana told *i-D* in June 2014.

LanaVision

Lana has more than 16 million subscribers on YouTube and amassed more than 6.5 billion views across 45 videos. These are her 10 most popular, ordered by viewing numbers:

1. 'Young and Beautiful' – 655 million views!

2. 'Born to Die'

3. 'Summertime Sadness'

4. 'Blue Jeans'

5. 'Video Games'

6. 'Don't Call Me Angel'

7. 'Love'

8. 'Lust For Life'

9. 'West Coast'

10. 'Ride'

"Family members will come on the road with me and say: 'Wow, your life is just like a movie!' And I'm like: 'Yeah, a really fucked-up movie.'"

Lana Del Rey, *Guardian*, June 2014

Coachella on My Mind

Since her first gig in 2011, Lana has performed at more than 78 festivals, and more than 400 live shows across six world tours.

Lana's most acclaimed shows, however, are her two iconic performances at Coachella. In 2014, she closed the festival on the final day on the Outdoor Stage. Precisely 10 years later in 2024, she was the headline act on the Main Stage.

For the 2024 performance, Lana entered the stage riding a motorcycle and was joined by special guest stars John Baptiste, Camila Cabello and Billie Eilish. Lana and Eilish sang two songs together – 'Ocean Eyes' and 'Video Games'.

"A lot of my songs are not just simple verse-chorus pop songs – they're more psychological."

Lana Del Rey, *Guardian*, June 2014

Released on 18 September 2015, Lana's fourth studio album *Honeymoon* is a masterpiece, receiving wild acclaim from fans and critics. It even features Lana's rather incredible attempt at a James Bond theme song, the track '24'.

***Honeymoon* blends together Lana's dreamy, baroque pop voice with smoky, sinister jazz while dark lyrical themes unveil a longing for an America that never existed. What song gives you the chills?**

Essential Album #3:

Honeymoon

1. 'Honeymoon'
2. 'Music to Watch Boys To'
3. 'Terrence Loves You'
4. 'God Knows I Tried'
5. 'High by the Beach'
6. 'Freak'
7. 'Art Deco'
8. 'Burnt Norton'
9. 'Religion'
10. 'Salvatore'
11. 'The Blackest Day'
12. '24'
13. 'Swan Song'
14. 'Don't Let Me Be Misunderstood'

23 July 2011

The day Amy Winehouse, Lana's musical hero, passed away was also the same day Lana received her first proper press review for 'Video Games'. She was travelling to Glasgow by train when she heard the news: "I had 10 seconds of the most elated feeling and then the news everywhere, on all of the televisions, was that Amy had died on her front steps and I was like 'NO!' I personally felt like I didn't even want to sing anymore," she told *Mojo* in June 2024.

The Sad Queen of Spotify

With more than 60 million monthly visitors – *and more than 30 billion total streams* – Lana is one of the most popular artists on the global streaming platform. These are her 10 most-played tracks:

1. 'Summertime Sadness' – 1.6 billion views!

2. 'Young and Beautiful'

3. 'Say Yes to Heaven'

4. 'West Coast'

5. 'Tough'

6. 'Cinnamon Girl'

7. 'Video Games'

8. 'Diet Mountain Dew'

9. 'Brooklyn Baby'

10. 'White Mustang'

Taylor X Lana

In 2022, Lana and Taylor Swift collaborated on 'Snow on the Beach', a song about two people falling in love at the same time. It's taken from Swift's multi-platinum *Midnights* (2022) record.

It's a good track, but after its release Lana's fans complained that she doesn't feature on it that much – just half a verse. Something had to be done. "I had no idea I was the only feature on that song. Had I known, I would have sung the entire second verse like Taylor wanted," Lana told *Billboard* in February 2024.

To remedy the situation, Lana and Taylor returned to the studio and added more Lana! The end result is much better.

“I’ve watched as one of my favourite artists of the decade, Lana Del Rey, be ruthlessly criticized early in her career, and then slowly but surely, she turned into, in my opinion, the most influential artist in pop. Her vocal stylings, her lyrics, her aesthetics: they’ve been echoed and repurposed everywhere in music. I just think she’s the best we’ve ever had.”

Taylor Swift, on Lana, *Uproxx*, December 2019

Published Author

In September 2020, Lana published her debut collection of poetry and photography entitled *Violet Bent Backwards over the Grass*. It features 19 poems, 10 haikus and at-home photographs.

Lana's desire to publish her poetry in book form, and as a spoken word album, came at a time during the recording of *Norman Fucking Rockwell* when the singer was creatively stuck. "It's kind of random," she told *The Fader* of the poetry collection in June 2019. "But it's been really cool for me, because I was having writer's block with the music and so I just sat down to write some words without music and I realized there was just a couple of things I wanted to say through some poems, which is funny. I feel like I'm in the 19th century."

The poetry collection was a big success and became a *New York Times* bestseller.

"I was always an unusual girl. My mother told me I had a chameleon soul. No moral compass pointing due north, no fixed personality. Just an inner indecisiveness that was as wide and as wavering as the ocean."

Lana Del Rey, *The Fader*, June 2014

Essential Album #4:

Lust for Life

1. 'Love'
2. 'Lust for Life'
3. '13 Beaches'
4. 'Cherry'
5. 'White Mustang'
6. 'Summer Bummer'
7. 'Groupie Love'
8. 'In My Feelings'
9. 'Coachella – Woodstock in My Mind'
10. 'God Bless America – And All the Beautiful Women in It'
11. 'When the World Was at War We Kept Dancing'
12. 'Beautiful People Beautiful Problems'
13. 'Tomorrow Never Came'
14. 'Heroin'
15. 'Change'
16. 'Get Free'

"I made my first four albums for me, but this one is for my fans and about where I hope we are all headed," Lana told *NME* regarding her fifth studio album, released on 21 July 2017.

Indeed, *Lust for Life* is Lana's longest and most ambitious album to date and definitely one for the fans. It sees the singer sharing the mic with big-hitting collaborators such as The Weeknd ('Lust for Life'), A$AP Rocky ('Summer Bummer' and 'Groupie Love'), Stevie Nicks ('Beautiful People Beautiful Problems') and Sean Ono Lennon ('Tomorrow Never Came').

The album proves beyond a doubt that when it comes to melodic anthems, Lana can pop as loud as her peers.

Soda Pop

Lana's lyrics are littered with lines that reference the great iconography of American popular culture. No more so is this true than when Lana references fizzy soda in her songs. In 'American Whore', Lana mentions 'A&W' root beer. In 'Cherry' and 'Wild at Heart', she references Coca-Cola, in 'Bartender' she croons about Cherry Coke, and in 'Cola' she sings about Pepsi.

"I am definitely chasing my own little American Dream."

Lana Del Rey, *Clash Music*, June 2014

"If I get a great melody in my head, I know it's a gift."

Lana Del Rey, *Pitchfork*, July 2017

This is the number of fans that saw Lana perform at Foro Sol stadium, Mexico City, in August 2023 – her highest ever capacity sold-out solo headlining show.

Lana played 23 songs, and came out on stage wearing a white bridal dress, and a veil adorned with red roses and black bows held in place with a tiara. "Believe me, the pleasure is all mine!" the visibly moved singer said as she sang her last song, 'Hope Is a Dangerous Thing for a Woman Like Me to Have – But I Have It'.

Literary Lover

Many of Lana's most profound lyrics contain references to her favourite films and literature, a collection of art so eclectic it could only swirl inside an artist like Lana. The singer is an avid reader and over the years has revealed her favourite novels. So, for your reading pleasure, here are Lana's reading pleasures:

1. *Lolita*, Vladimir Nabokov (1955)
2. *Leaves of Grass*, Walt Whitman (1855)
3. *The Road to Paradise Island*, Victoria Holt (1985)
4. *Think and Grow Rich*, Napoleon Hill (1937)
5. *The Bell Jar*, Sylvia Plath (1963)
6. *Howl and Other Poems*, Allen Ginsberg (1956)
7. *The Master Key System*, Charles F. Haanel (1916)
8. *Forbidden Gates*, Thomas Horn (2010)
9. *Your Erroneous Zones*, Wayne Dyer (1976)
10. *Hollywood Babylon*, Kenneth Anger (1959)
11. *Autobiography of a Yogi*, Paramahansa Yogananda (1946)

"I did not foresee the amount of chaos and confusion there would be when I became well known."

Lana Del Rey, *NME*, December 2015

Chapter Three

Ultra Fucking Cool

Glastonbury Set List

1. 'Nature Boy'
2. 'A&W'
3. 'Young and Beautiful'
4. 'Bartender'
5. 'The Grants'
6. 'Cherry'
7. 'Pretty When You Cry'
8. 'Ride'
9. 'Born to Die'
10. 'Blue Jeans'
11. 'Norman Fucking Rockwell'
12. 'Arcadia'
13. 'Candy Necklace'
14. 'Ultraviolence'
15. 'White Mustang'
16. 'Video Games'

Time's Up

"Damn, this is a big crowd!" Lana yelled upon walking out to her Glastonbury 2024 performance on the Other Stage, a set as infamous as it is iconic.

Lana arrived 30 minutes late to the stage ("due to make-up and hair") and then, controversially, had the plug pulled by the organizers when she broke the 11.45 p.m. curfew – with five songs left to play. "I've heard of curfews before but I didn't know they actually turned the lights off," she told the *Sunday Times* in December 2024.

"Every so often, I top what I've done, and this video is definitely the most beautiful thing I've ever done. I wrote a treatment for me and A$AP Rocky, because I just thought he'd be really perfect to star in it."

Lana Del Rey, *Huffington Post*, June 2012

National Anthem

Lana's love of the rapper A$AP Rocky (partner of Rihanna) is well known. She has often cited him as her favourite rapper, collaborating with him more than any other artist to date, and more is expected to follow. Lana first featured on Rocky's 'Ridin'' and 'National Anthem', both in 2012, as well as 2017's 'Summer Bummer' and 'Groupie Love'.

The eight-minute video of 'National Anthem' in which the duo portray Jacqueline Kennedy Onassis and John F. Kennedy is as wild as it wonderful – and has amassed more than 105 million views.

Super Mario!

Lana's favourite video game is *Mario Kart*. Her "unfavourite" (her word) video game is *World of Warcraft*, the game that inspired her debut hit song 'Video Game'. Her boyfriend at the time would play the game for hours every day after work and not let Lana join in.

World of Warcraft remains the biggest-selling massively multiplayer online role-playing game (MMORPG) of all time with tens of millions sold.

"I love my records. I love them. I'm proud of the way I've put parts of my story into songs in ways that only I understand."

Lana Del Rey, *W* magazine, February 2018

The Godfather of Movies

Lana's favourite movies of all time, *The Godfather* and *The Godfather Part II*, were directed by Francis Ford Coppola in 1972 and 1974 respectively. Today they are, without a doubt, among the most influential icons of American culture and cinema and are regularly voted the greatest movies ever made.

"I'm obsessed with them both, not just because of the storyline and the actors but also the settings," Lana told *Far Out*, in September 2023. "I love the sets for both movies; they're very luxurious and gorgeous and they just have the most epic acting of all time."

She also told *Discopop* in January 2012, "It's not the darkness I'm attracted to, it's the fact that it's so visually stunning."

"I was sort of a late bloomer with style. Part of my retro sensibility comes from my love of old movies from when I was a teenager. I remember seeing films like *A Place in the Sun* with Elizabeth Taylor or films with Natalie Wood and thinking that they were so beautiful. But as much as I loved 1950s films, I loved '60s music – and still do above any genre."

Lana Del Rey, *W* magazine, February 2018

The G.O.A.T.

In 2023, *Rolling Stone* magazine ranked Lana 175 on its iconic list of the 200 Greatest Singers of All Time.

In the list, Lana was sandwiched between Buddy Holly (174) and Iggy Pop (176) – two vastly different American icons that represent both the wilder side of music and the more wholesome – the fine line Lana herself attempts to walk.

In the same year, *Rolling Stone* UK named Lana the Greatest American Songwriter of the 21st century, beating Taylor Swift, Lady Gaga, Miley Cyrus and Beyoncé.

"I never wanted to lead a normal life."

Lana Del Rey, GQ, October 2012

"I'm not just one thing. I'm not cheerful all the time. But being able to express my sadness sometimes makes me actually more cheerful than some people I know, because I gave myself permission to have a lot of colours."

Lana Del Rey, *NME*, September 2019

Queen of Sadcore

Lana was crowned "Queen of Sadcore" in 2011. However, the neologism dates back to 2006 when Cat Power first obtained the title.

Lana was given the label in part due to her contralto vocal range, a lower singing register than most of her contemporaries, and relatively rare among female pop singers.

Lana began singing predominantly in contralto while recording *Born to Die*. "People weren't taking me very seriously, so I lowered my voice, believing that it would help me stand out," she told the *Daily Star* in November 2011.

Norman Fucking Rockwell

Norman Rockwell, the inspiration behind the title track of Lana's highly acclaimed fifth album of the same name (bar the expletive, of course!), was an acclaimed American painter and illustrator whose work became important during the Second World War.

Rockwell's representations of Americana – and American values – especially through his work for the *Saturday Evening Post*, where he created more than 300 cover illustrations from 1916–1963, made him a beloved symbol of America's virtues.

In true Lana fashion, *NFR* – as it is known – is less about America's virtues and more about its vices, and how one can't exist without the other.

At the 2020 Grammy Awards, the album received two nominations, including the prestigious Album of the Year, and was ranked 321 in *Rolling Stone*'s 500 Greatest Albums of All Time.

"I knew they were going to like *Norman Fucking Rockwell* – there's nothing not to like about it."

Lana Del Rey, *Mojo*, June 2023

Chuck Grant

Lana's not the only gifted creative in her family. Her younger sister, Caroline AKA Chuck, is a talented photographer, responsible for several of Lana's album covers and promotional photo shoots, alongside long-term photographer Neil Krug.

It was Chuck who photographed the cover for 2019's *Norman Fucking Rockwell*. Alongside Lana, the cover features Duke Nicholson, the grandson of legendary actor Jack Nicholson, posing on a sailboat – the second cover of Lana's to feature a boat after 'High by the Beach' (2015).

"People said I came from money. It was really tough to get over some stigma of this idea of having my dad buying my album and giving me a record deal and us being some rich white family when we fought over money constantly when we were young. I was not from the right side of the tracks, period."

Lana Del Rey, *Mojo*, June 2023

“I was introduced to Liverpool FC by my manager whose mood is dependent on the Liverpool results. Liverpool are my team – I love watching Luis Suárez play.”

Lana Del Rey, *Metro*, March 2013

The Reds

Lana is an avid Liverpool FC fan and has been since 2009 when her British manager, Ben Mawson, began taking her to games at Anfield Stadium when Lana lived in the UK from 2010–12.

To prove she's a fan, Lana released a limited-edition single of the club's anthem 'You'll Never Walk Alone' for a documentary about the team called *The End of the Storm*, with all profits of the single going to Liverpool's charity foundation.

Lana Del Rey-core

In 2024, Pinterest saw a 300 per cent rise in searches for "Lana Dey Rey-core" – as users searched for fashion inspo from the songstress and fans argued about whether her style could be classified as a "core".

Her ultrafeminine romantic aesthetic, heavy on the 1950s and '60s glamour, comprises vintage clothing, A-line dresses, floaty fabric, pearls, thick eyeliner and bouffant hair – and has been pretty constant throughout her stardom. That said, she's just as likely to be papped in jeans and a baggy tee.

"Lana Del Rey – she just stabs my soul all the time and makes me just want to cry. I love how mysterious she is as well. And I love that she just puts a record out and that's it."

Adele, *New York Times*, December 2015.

"I didn't even get famous 'til I was 27. Until then, I sang for less than free. And I loved it. I really was that girl who was pure of soul. I didn't give a fuck."

Lana Del Rey, *Mojo*, June 2023

True Love

For several years, Lana has spoken of her desire to have a "dominant male in my life that is hands-on" and "escape through a really passionate romance" (*Style*, May 2013). She has also frequently been seen wearing white bridal gowns and veils on stage and in photo shoots.

On 26 September 2024, Lana's dream came true. At the age of 39, she married Jeremy Dufrene, an alligator tour boat captain, by the water in Des Allemands, Louisiana. Lana met "my guy", a divorced father of three, after she took a boat tour with him and some friends in 2019.

On the day she said "I do", Lana wore a long white dress with a light blue satin bow in her hair and walked down the aisle with her father Robert Grant by her side.

Ghetto Monégasque

Lana's iconic and highly stylized look is a large part of her identity with her fans. As quoted in *Vogue* 2011, Lana describes her individual style as "Ghetto Monégasque" (Monaco Ghetto) or a poor's man idea of wealthy – mixing the supremely artful bouffant hair and doll-like lashes of her idols such as Veronica Lake, Lauren Bacall and Sophia Loren, with faded vintage tees and sundresses for a more modern twist.

"I don't really have any gimmicks. I don't actually do anything that's strange. I don't even wear weird things. I have been taking my music to labels for years, and everyone just thought it was creepy. They thought the images with the music were weird and verging on psychotic. And then, one day, people decided it wasn't actually too strange. You know what changed? It got played on the radio."

Lana Del Rey, *The Daily Telegraph*, January 2012

Chapter Four

A Happy Kind of Sad

"I think *Born to Die* is gorgeous. If it sounds like everything fits perfectly together, it's because it does. There is nothing altered, nothing compromised, they are perfectly me. For better or worse, this album is me in song form."

Lana Del Rey, *The Daily Telegraph*, January 2012

In August 2020, Lana learned that one of her greatest influences, and perhaps the most enduring icon of American popular culture – Bruce Springsteen – is one of her biggest fans. Springsteen heaped gushing praise on Lana on his SiriusXM show in August 2020, telling his listeners:

"Lana is from New York, and was raised in Lake Placid, a fabulous little American town where I have spent many a lovely summer evening with my children and my family over the years. Lana is simply one of the best songwriters in the country, as we speak. She just creates a world of her own and invites you in. So a big favourite of mine, the lovely Lana Del Rey."

"If I had realized just how many people were gonna watch 'Video Games' then I would have had my hair and make-up done. And maybe I wouldn't have shot it on my laptop!"

Lana Del Rey, *i-D*, June 2014

Woman of the Year

In 2012, Lana posed on the front cover of *GQ*'s October issue to celebrate being crowned as the magazine's prestigious Woman of the Year, all thanks to the global success of *Born to Die*. "Just to have someone acknowledge the material I write is incredibly touching," Lana said at the formal ceremony, attended by many of the world's greatest, and most stylish, icons. "It's an affirmation of sorts. I just didn't think that this was going to happen. Not any of it." Model Lara Stone won the award the year before and actor Emma Watson won the following year.

"As a child, I felt different. I always wanted to make my life a work of art."

Lana Del Rey, *Glamour*, January 2013

Poolside

In June 2010, Lana let down her hair and starred in her debut short film, *Poolside*, directed by friend, Aaron Peer. The film follows Ray and JP who work their summers cleaning the pools of wealthy families.

One day, Ray becomes fascinated with the private lives of one of his clients, particularly Lisa (portrayed by Lana, dressed mainly in a black swimsuit), the daughter of an affluent client.

Shot over a weekend on a budget of $400 in Seaside Heights, New Jersey, the 12-minute film premiered in June 2012, a year after Lana found global fame. A remastered 2024 edit is now available to view on YouTube.

The Right Person Will Stay

Lana's tenth studio album, *The Right Person Will Stay*, was released on 21 May 2025, after months of anticipation, delays and title changes.

The 13-track album was announced in November 2024 on Lana's Insta, along with the news that the lead single will be 'Henry'. The announcement received more than 3 million likes in its first 24 hours.

Alongside the revelation of the album's release, Lana also revealed the five dates of her 2025 UK and Ireland stadium tour, including her first-ever headline stadium date at London's iconic 90,000-capacity Wembley Stadium in July 2025.

"I wasn't even born in the '50s but I feel like I was there."

Lana Del Rey, *Artistdirect*, February 2016

353 million

The total number of views 'Video Games' has on YouTube. More interestingly, the video has more than 70,000 comments, many of which seemingly speak of how poignant and powerful the song remains after all these years, no doubt due to the chorus's heartbreaking refrain – "Heaven is a place on earth with you".

"I'm super grateful for my managers Ben [Mawson] and Ed [Millett]. They picked me out of the bar scenes, lounge singer scenes that I was singing in for eight years before I met them. They got me out of a deal I made for 11 records for $10,000 while I was working at a restaurant and living in a trailer park. Ben did that in one hour and then the next day he flew me to London and let me live with him. In a year, I wrote 'Video Games' and I was ready to make good records. I was ready to make a lot of records."

Lana Del Rey, acceptance speech, Variety Hitmakers Decade Award, December 2021

Bond Girl?

In May 2024, Lana revealed to her fans that the track '24' from her 2015 album *Honeymoon* was submitted to the producers of the *James Bond* movies for consideration to be the opening credit theme for *Spectre*, the 24th film in the superspy film franchise. "I wrote '24' for them", Lana said.

Unfortunately, Lana lost out to Sam Smith's 'Writing's on the Wall'. That song went on to win an Academy Award for Best Original Song.

"Sam, you did a wonderful job", Lana said to congratulate Smith.

"I'm as different as I am the same. Which is hugely different and hugely the same, in a creative aspect. Singing is a real calling for me, but the rest of my life is like... sheesh. I'm surprised by how much it changes all the time."

Lana Del Rey, *NME*, September 2019

Del Rey All Day

"Billie's my girl, it makes me feel comforted that music is going in such a good direction," Lana told *Billboard* in February 2023 about Billie Eilish, an artist in debt to Lana's path clearing. Billie's not the only one, however. You can hear Lana's influence all over these hits...

1. **'New Americana' – Halsey**
2. **'I'm A Ruin' – Marina and the Diamonds**
3. **'Hollywood Forever Cemetery Sings' – Father John Misty**
4. **'Glory and Gore' – Lorde**
5. **'You're Not the One' – Sky Ferreira**
6. **'Break the Rules' – Charli XCX**
7. **'Good to Love' – FKA Twigs**
8. **'Childs Play' – SZA**
9. **'Eventually' – Tame Impala**
10. **'Loner' – Kali Uchis**

"I don't want to hear that Billie Eilish is the new Lana Del Rey. Do not disrespect Lana like that! That woman has made her brand so perfect for her whole career and shouldn't have to hear that."

Billie Eilish, *Los Angeles Times*, April 2019

Kimye

On 24 May 2014, Lana embraced her newfound fame when she accepted Kanye West's invitation to perform at his wedding to Kim Kardashian. West was a huge fan of Lana's. At the ceremony, Lana sang 'Young and Beautiful', 'Summertime Sadness' and 'Blue Jeans', before leaving.

In October 2018, Lana distanced herself from her association with Kanye after the controversial rapper publicly endorsed Donald Trump. "I can only assume you relate to his personality on some level," Lana wrote on Twitter (now X). "Delusions of grandeur, extreme issues with narcissism. If you think it's alright to support someone who believes it's OK to grab a woman just because he's famous then you need an intervention just as much as he does."

"I don't think I'll write another record. What would I say? I feel like everything I wanted to say, I've said already. *Born to Die* is a tribute to living life on the wild side. I'm sort of kidding because I'm not that wild any more... used to drink a lot. Too much. I haven't had a drink for seven years now."

Lana Del Rey, *Vogue*, October 2012

"As soon as it flew out of my manager's mouth, it fucking stuck like glue."

Lana Del Rey, *NME*, May 2014

Gangsta Nancy

"I spend eight fucking years writing gorgeous songs and someone in a meeting says 'Gangsta Nancy Sinatra' and that's that." Lana told the *NME* in May 2014. Lana was speaking, of course, about the comparison of her that went viral soon after she became famous. (Indeed, if you now Google the phrase "Gangsta Nancy Sinatra" all searches lean toward Lana!)
It was supposed to be a joke, but the phrase still hounds Lana even now.

Thankfully, in April 2012, Nancy Sinatra herself responded to the likeness, posting on Twitter: "Sad that Lana Del Rey got stuck with that 'Gangsta Nancy' thing. Not true. Unfair to her. She's her own person."

Grammy Incoming?

In 10 years at the top of the music industry, Lana has won a multitude of high-profile awards, most notably a prestigious Ivor Novello Award for Best Contemporary Song for 'Video Games' (2012), an ASCAP Global Impact Award (2018) and a Golden Globe for 'Big Eyes' (2014).

In fact, the only thing missing from Lana's trophy cabinet is a Grammy Award – she has received 11 nominations but never won. Can *The Right Person Will Stay* break the curse?

"There's nothing anyone could ever tell me that I don't already know. I know everything about myself. I know why I do what I do. All of my compulsions and interests and inspirations. I'm very in sync with that."

Lana Del Rey, *Rolling Stone*, July 2014

Lanatics

The nickname of Lana's fans.

Unfortunately, several of Lana's fans have lived up to their name. Since 2015, Lana has faced several deeply invasive moments involving fans, including a teenage male who camped out in the garage of her Malibu home, the theft of two of her Jaguars (cars, not the cat), as well as two Russian teenagers who have left violent, threatening, suicidal letters in her mailbox.

"In short: all the scary shit," Lana told *Pitchfork* in July 2017. "I've had people in my house for sure, and I didn't know they were there while I was there. I had a hard time sleeping for a minute."

"My publicists, in their long career, say they have never seen someone be more fictionalized."

Lana Del Rey, BBC News, January 2012

Most Influential

In December 2021, iconic US trade magazine *Variety* honoured Lana at their famous Hitmakers Decade Awards ceremony, for being one of the most influential singer-songwriters of the 21st century. The award is a cherished prize given to a select few. Harry Styles and BTS are the most recent recipients.

Lana's acceptance speech was emotional, ending, of course, with pure Lana-esque poetry: "I always like to say that the way I live my life is my poetry, my lovemaking is my legacy, and I get to make music in between."

Greatest Hits (That Feel Like a Kiss)

To celebrate the release of Lana's ninth studio album *Did You Know That There's a Tunnel Under Ocean Blvd*, in March 2023, *Rolling Stone* ranked the 50 greatest Lana Del Rey songs (out of the 130+ she has recorded). Do you agree with their Top 20?

A Happy Kind of Sad

20. 'Music to Watch Boys To'
19. 'Summertime Sadness'
18. 'Cherry'
17. 'Blue Jeans'
16. 'Ultraviolence'
15. 'A&W'
14. 'National Anthem'
13. 'Young and Beautiful'
12. 'Mariners Apartment Complex'
11. 'Hope Is A Dangerous Thing For A Woman Like Me To Have – But I Have It'
10. 'Born to Die'
9. 'Venice Bitch'
8. 'Brooklyn Baby'
7. 'High by the Beach'
6. 'Ride'
5. 'Off to the Races'
4. 'Norman Fucking Rockwell'
3. 'West Coast'
2. 'The Greatest'
1. 'Video Games'

"Hope truly is a dangerous thing for a woman like me to have, because I know so much. But I have it."

Lana Del Rey, *Billboard*, August 2019